Praise for The Healer's Journey...

"Ernesto's book should be made mandatory for all newly licensed massage therapists. Being an LMT for twelve years, I still find it very informative and useful." *-- Vivian Madison, LMT*
Past FSMTA Insurance Chair,
Author of **FSMTA Insurance Reimbursement Manual**

"A book that all massage teachers, directors and owners would benefit from...All too often massage educators mistake education and training as also being sufficient mentoring and supervision...Ernesto Fernandez has done a good job offering clear and thought-provoking suggestions."
-- Benny Vaughn, LMT, ATC
Massage Educator, Certified Athletic Trainer,
recipient of 1996 FSMTA International
Achievement Award

"Informative, practical needed information to expand therapists' understanding and communication with their clients. Necessary reading for all therapists looking to expand their skills."
-- Gloria Carlson, LMT
President FSMTA-Broward Chapter

"When I first read your book, my first feeling was one of guilt. For twenty-three years I've been an LMT and I've always been afraid to share with any other LMT for fear that it might cost me something. I was wrong. After reading this book I'm only sorry I missed all the wonderful opportunities Ernesto has shown me...Thank you for opening my eyes to mentoring."

D1416745

"This book should be a required text in every massage therapy school."   **-- Herbert Levin, LMT**
                                          Professional Massage Educator

"*The Healer's Journey* should be a required text for...the health care field...Having been a professor, instructor, mentor and supervisor to thousands of health care professionals over the past thirty years, I only wish I had been as well prepared as Ernesto Fernandez to supply the best guidelines, training supervision and evaluation...This book was a monumental task, extremely well illustrated."
                                  -- Aaron Mattes, MS, RKT, LMT
                                  Professional Massage Educator,
                          Creator of Active Isolated Stretching

"A special study of the relationship between massage therapists and their mentors...The product of several years of personal experience with mentoring in the massage field, as both a giver and a receiver of inspiration and wisdom."
                                        -- Steve Capellini, LMT
                                Author of The Massage Business

The
Healer's
Journey

**Transforming Your Bodywork Career
Through Mentoring and Supervision**

Second Edition

Ernesto J. Fernandez

MA, LMHC, LMT

R B
Roldan-Bauta
PRESS

14715 Tall Tree Drive
Lutz, FL 33549

Printed in the United States of America

ISBN 0-9661928-1-8

Dedication

I dedicate this book to my partner Andrea,
who *literally* supported me,
so I could complete this book.

Acknowledgements

Two individuals have given much of themselves in the writing of this book. I am grateful to Stephen D'Andrea and Andrea Hummel for their friendship, encouragement and endless hours of editing.

Special thanks go to Don McCann and Dallas Hancock for being my teachers, mentors, and friends for the past thirteen years. They have helped me evolve into who I am professionally.

Above all, thanks to all the massage therapists who have trusted me with their pain, disappointments and triumphs in pursuit of their passion. They inspired me to write this book and teach this material.

E.J.F.
Lutz, Florida
July 1997

Contents

A Parable

Often, young birds set out from their nests too early. Their wings are not fully developed and they are not strong enough to fly. What happens? They fall and crash to the earth.

Once they crash, they keep hobbling along. Their vision is not very clear and their hunting skills are not good. After all, they are birds. So they crawl among the roots, looking for insects and worms to survive on, and risk getting eaten by wild animals.

Many do not know how to make a nest for themselves to keep warm, so a good number do not survive. Their survival depends on whether they are able to find nourishment and build their strength. Even if they live, their growth is stunted.

And so it takes them a long time before they fly the way they are designed to, soaring effortlessly through the sky.

Introduction

Fledgling massage therapists are much like birds. They relish the warm nurturing "nest" of massage school surrounded by others just like them. But when, at graduation, they must leave and set out into the sky on their own, they face the daunting test of flying solo.

Luckily, massage therapists differ from birds in one important way -- they do not have to "eat worms" to survive. They can reach out to others for help, guidance and further training. They, too, can soar through the world the way they are designed to -- if only they are willing to reach out for help.

Since I became a massage therapist in 1987, I have observed the rapid evolution of the massage and bodywork profession in the United States. Increased recognition as health care providers, acceptance by insurance companies, and new research supporting the validity of our work has benefited therapists.

The profession has also expanded into many new directions with a diversity of manual manipulation treatment methods such as craniosacral work, chair massage, visceral manipulation, lymphatic drainage, and myofascial release. These methods are currently being used with broad applications in a new variety of contexts (e.g. health spas, medical clinics, hospitals, airports, athletic events).

In other words, our profession is evolving very rapidly. We are sought out by clients to help relieve stress and pain, and collectively have done so successfully for many years.

> *Each bodyworker and massage therapist has a contribution to make to the profession and the community. They touch many people's lives in a positive way.*

At the same time, over the past nine years I have heard numerous massage therapists and bodyworkers express their concern that *there is no community or support system* in place to help support therapists with the many issues faced as independent health care practitioners. The irony is that we are professional caregivers, caring for and serving clients all day, yet *we have not learned how to serve each other.*

There is no support system for massage therapists for expressing and working through fears, confusions, concerns, struggles and mistakes. Bodyworkers who have the financial resources typically get their support needs met by: a) taking a massage workshop (but who do you consult with for feedback and support between workshops?); b) getting counseling or psychotherapy (which still cannot improve your massage techniques); or c) receiving bodywork from an experienced massage therapist in the community (which is sometimes coupled with informal mentoring).

Massage therapists who do not have the financial means to afford a regular diet of massage workshops, counseling, or quality bodywork, remain marginally involved in the profession, often doing massage part-time while working a day job.

In my ten years of bodywork and counseling I have experienced and witnessed the triumphs and pitfalls of becoming a successful and effective massage therapist. In my development as a massage therapist and as a mental health counselor, I was very fortunate to have a mentor and supervisor who was both a massage therapist and a mental health counselor, a person who understood how to integrate the roles and skills of both professions.

I am certain that without the mentoring relationship I had with Don McCann during the first six years of my career, it would have been more difficult for me to achieve my current professional goals.

Yet even with this kind of support, my path was arduous and at times bewildering. I have experienced what isolation, burnout, and an open heart can do to a bodyworker. I personally encountered numerous periods of doubt, financial problems, health challenges, anxiety and depression.

What helped me heal during these difficult periods was my commitment to seeking out and consulting my mentors.

Over the years, I collected stories and experiences from: a) massage therapists I treated as clients for bodywork, counseling and emotional release work,   b) informal conversations, discussions and interviews with massage

15

therapists, school owners, and educators I met in the community, in my travels, and in workshops, c) participants in my own workshops and lectures, d) state and national professional association officers I worked with as education standards chair, and e) association members who called me with their own questions, challenges, tragedies and concerns.

It is from these experiences of other bodyworkers that I identified and defined six categories of obstacles which bodyworkers face in their journey of pursuing private practice and working with people in pain. These are obstacles that mentors can help beginning practitioners overcome. I refer to them as the *six competencies* of the massage and bodywork profession. They are:

- Massage Therapy Skills and Professional Identity
- The Therapeutic Relationship
- Self-Promotion
- Business Management
- Personal Empowerment
- Social Support

The issues comprising these competencies are almost always present for therapists, whether we are currently focusing on them or not. In addition, when we master the issues in a given competency we are not finished with them; we usually cycle through and revisit those same issues again and again as we mature in our careers.

In this book only the two clinical competencies (massage therapy skills and professional identity; and the therapeutic relationship) are addressed. Additional books are needed in our profession to discuss the remaining four competencies.

I believe mentoring and supervision is the most effective method for mastering all of these competencies, hence the topic of this book.

Part One discusses the benefits of mentoring, how to find support, how to be an effective mentor or mentee, and what issues to work on via this professional relationship.

Part Two goes into more depth on the two clinical competencies that lend themselves to exploration through mentoring. The seasoned professional may ask his mentee to pursue additional training and examine her professional identity. He may also work with his protege to transform her client relationships from service-based ones to fully therapeutic ones.

I have found that self-reliant, prosperous and self-confident massage therapists had someone who supported them in reaching their professional aspirations. Those who did not feel satisfied with their professional and financial achievements never sought out or had a mentor.

My intent for you, the reader, is to empower you to break the silence, end the isolation and advance your career by:

• Working with an appropriate mentor or supervisor
• Creating your own peer support system with other
  massage therapists
• Developing a positive professional identity. (Being a
  massage therapist involves much more than we are given
  credit for.)

- Identifying and avoiding common pitfalls of becoming a massage therapist
- Mentoring or supervising another massage therapist
- Exploring the six competencies of the massage therapy profession.

This book is intended for bodyworkers and massage therapists, massage therapy school staff and their students, employers, continuing education providers, officers of professional associations, and anyone considering massage therapy as a career.

PART ONE: THE MENTORING RELATIONSHIP

Chapter 1

Constructing the Model

To begin breaking the silence, I researched supervision models used in other health professions. I did not want to assume that the process my own mentor Don McCann and I were using was the most appropriate or effective method for mentoring and supervising massage therapists.

This journey led me to review Florida Statutes regulating other health professions. I reviewed their trade journals and association literature and interviewed countless practitioners.

I sought information on structures for supervision during training and supervision post-training. I asked practitioners what they found helpful about the supervision they received, what (if anything) could be done differently, and whether the structure was effective.

Professions I examined were: primary care physicians (osteopathic, chiropractic, and orthopedic); mental health (counseling, social work, marriage and family, and psychologists); and allied health (physical and occupational therapy, and nursing).

Next, I put into context all the information I had gathered. I compared these health professions to the massage therapy profession with regard to the following variables:

- average length of treatment/consultations
- range of treatment types (modalities, therapies)
- level of professional intimacy with the client/patient
- technical level of treatments
- length of formal and advanced training required
- potential for injury to the patient as a result of treatment.

What I found was that the massage therapy profession has more in common with the mental health professions than with medical professions, regarding:

- average length of treatment/consultation (medium to long, meaning 30-90 minute sessions)
- range of treatment types (modalities, therapies)
- level of professional intimacy with the client/patient (high)
- technical level of treatments (low-tech).

For this reason, the model I developed for mentoring and supervision in the massage therapy and bodywork profession draws heavily on models used in mental health professions.

The massage profession differed from all health professions (including mental health) on the length of formal and advanced training required.[1] Other allied health professions also had similarities to massage therapy except that the average length of treatment was much shorter.

Massage therapy is the only profession (other than mental health professions) that typically finds practitioners spending an hour or longer with an individual in an intimate professional relationship. I believe what we do is even more intimate because we are touching people who are semi-nude. Since we spend just as much time with clients as mental health professionals do, we are subject to the same kind of issues that affect them. These include transference, countertransference, isolation and burnout, to name just a few.

In addition, the mental health professions require at least three years of clinical supervision with another experienced mental health professional where they are groomed into competent and self-confident professionals -- before they even get licensed. We receive our licenses immediately, right after we finish massage school! I believe this sets newly licensed massage therapists up for disillusionment and financial struggle.

Massage therapists who have attained success without a professional support system deserve a lot of credit. But we need them to initiate the next generation of bodyworkers.

All people face an array of physical and emotional issues throughout their lives. Being a therapist does not protect us

---

[1] For example, while osteopaths and massage therapists perform many of the same manual therapies, osteopaths have 10-12 years of education and a larger scope of practice.

from dealing with human issues (e.g. depression, divorce, abuse, IRS problems, bankruptcy, foreclosure). Massage therapists will face inadvertent errors in clinical and therapeutic judgement (e.g. poor case management or injuring a client by breaking a rib).

Each bodyworker or massage therapist who does not succeed or drops out of active practice of massage therapy is a loss to our profession. Each time the community loses a tremendous resource.

Without mentoring, many massage therapists are ill-equipped to avoid burn-out from:

• *Physical challenges* such as physical burnout (repetitive strain injuries to their wrists, shoulders or back, which prevent them from doing massage), as well as physical illness (such as Chronic Fatigue Syndrome and Epstein-Barr Virus).

• *Psychosocial challenges* such as emotional burnout and compassion fatigue. Personal issues surfacing (internal "I'm not OK" messages, cycles of shame, fear and de-pression, co-dependency, substance abuse, past unre-solved traumas) and lack of support (a spouse or partner who feels insecure, jealous or threatened and withdraws support; a divorce that drains financial resources).

• *Business challenges* such as not being able to maintain cash flow to meet overhead or needing additional skills for successful self promotion.

When we openly discuss these issues without fear of reprisal, we feel less isolated and more validated and empowered to take positive action.

Chapter 2

Mentoring and Supervision Defined

Professional methods for advancing and developing the skills and competencies of massage therapists

What is mentoring?

The purpose of mentoring is:

> to promote the development of the learner...[resulting in] an increase in the ability to perceive and hold complexity, to tolerate ambiguity, to experience one's own and others' feelings more richly, to see oneself and others in a broader context, and to make wholehearted commitments in a complex, tentative, and interdependent world (Daloz, 1990, p. 206).

Mentors are individuals who:

> cultivate their students' growth, they don't "push" or "pull" so much as *align themselves in relation to*

their students. Their work is to empower their students by helping to draw out and give form to what their students already know. They call out the best parts of their students. They serve as midwives or guides rather than solely as sources of knowledge (Daloz, 1990, p. 206).

A person who works with a mentor is called a *protege,* a French word for "someone who is protected."

What is supervision?

It is usually defined as:

an intensive, interpersonally focused one-to-one relationship in which one person is designated to facilitate the development of therapeutic competence in the other person (Loganbill et al., 1982 p.4).

Supervision is also:

an intervention that is provided by a senior member of a profession to a junior member or members of the same profession. This relationship is evaluative, extends over time, and has the simultaneous purposes of enhancing the professional functioning of the junior member(s), monitoring the quality of professional services offered to the clients she, he or they see(s), and serving as a gatekeeper for those who are to enter the profession (Bernard and Goodyear, 1992, p. 4)

26

Supervision is a *distinct intervention,* much like massage therapy, colon hydrotherapy, and active isolated stretching.

A person who receives clinical supervision is called a *supervisee.*

Supervisors and supervisees should belong to the same profession, according to Bernard and Goodyear (1992), because supervision helps the supervisee to develop a professional identity, learn therapeutic and risk management skills and become socialized into the profession by role models.

In the massage therapy profession today, students receive various levels of supervision during their massage therapy training. However, *postgraduate* supervision is still very rare among practicing massage therapists.

The terms mentor and supervisor will be used somewhat interchangeably here, for the sake of simplicity. Be aware, however, that there are some differences between the two, as just explained. Likewise, the terms protege and supervisee will be used interchangeably.

How do education and training versus mentoring and supervision compare?

Similarities
- Both involve teaching and learning.
- Education, training and clinical supervision have an evaluative and gatekeeping function.
- Mentoring does not have an evaluative and gatekeeping function.

27

Differences   • Education and training has an explicit
curriculum and teaching goals.
• Mentoring and clinical supervision is
tailored to meet the unique needs of each
individual.

What should you expect from mentoring and supervision?

Several sources of information are used in the mentoring
and supervision process:

Self-reports   verbal or written reports by the
protege on his/her experience and
progress

SOAP notes   therapy notes taken during/after a
treatment

Live observation   supervisor observing a supervisee
performing specific techniques

Audio / video taping   recordings of a treatment session for
later review and feedback.

The massage therapist must have a client's informed
consent in order to discuss his/her case with a mentor or
supervisor -- unless the client remains anonymous in the
discussion.

In choosing any particular supervision method, consider the
following:

The supervisee's:
1. learning goals
2. experience level and developmental issues
3. learning style

The supervisor's:
4. goals for the supervise
5. theoretical orientation
6. own learning goals for the supervisory
   experience (Bernard and Goodyear, 1992).

Mentors and supervisors help their students by providing:

Information
- Sharing skills, knowledge, resource materials and
  an opportunity to develop and practice new skills.

Counseling
- Giving support, validation and encouragement
- Calling out the inner voice
- Identifying the protege's vision and purpose for
  pursuing massage therapy
- Listening attentively and providing a safe space to
  speak confidentially
- Giving validation that the supervisee is doing good
  work
- Being supportive during crisis in the protege's life
- Expressing positive expectations.

Guidance and advising
- Helping the student identify alternative
  perspectives, exploring options and opportunities,

and identifying treatment strategies.

Feedback and perspective
- Observing the massage therapist's verbal and behavioral skills
- Discussing perceptions, values, attitudes, feelings, personal issues, and ethical dilemmas
- Reviewing clients' treatment plans, SOAP notes and progress
- Focusing on refining, adapting and expanding the application of massage techniques and evaluation skills the student has already learned
- Providing a theoretical framework
- Identifying and maximizing strengths
- Addressing current issues and concerns in working with clients
- Identifying assumptions and generalizations that the supervisee makes.

Modeling
- Allowing live observation of the mentor using the verbal, behavioral and/or technical skills discussed.

Mirroring and reflection
- Building awareness
- Challenging the supervisee to face her blind spots
- Identifying projections and countertransference.

Individualized instruction
- Providing appropriate structure and tasks for skill development
- Role-playing
- Demonstrating and simulating skills
- Reviewing case studies

- Tutoring to review what has already been learned and building on this
- Suggesting new medical and technical terminology.

How can mentoring and supervision benefit the massage therapy profession?

Professional guidance can greatly enhance the profession as a whole by creating a safe, supportive, healing environment for the growth and development of massage therapists and the massage therapy profession. It can also create a supportive professional community that promotes the growth and well-being of massage therapists in service to their communities.

How can mentoring and supervision benefit you the massage therapy practitioner?

Supervisors help massage therapists function at a higher level, so they learn within the context of their own work experience. Mentors also share and teach extensive professional, industry and organizational knowledge relatively risk-free. They often know the professional pitfalls to avoid and are willing to provide supportive and blunt assessments of both individuals and situations. They openly reveal how therapeutic and business decisions are made, and may even be able to open doors and facilitate job opportunities for the supervisee.

Who can benefit from clinical supervision?

Supervision is recommended primarily for massage therapists whose treatment goals are to reduce physical or emotional pain, and facilitate healing and rehabilitation. These interventions may take the form of injury/pain rehabilitation, emotional release work with mental health issues, or somatic education for the relief and healing of chronic symptoms and dysfunctions. Supervision is especially important for bodyworkers who are billing insurance and co-treating with physicians.

Mentoring is vital for the beginning massage therapist and beneficial throughout one's career. Even experienced professionals should seek out mentoring when faced with challenges in their careers.

Chapter 3

The Effective Mentor

What qualities to look for and how to be a quality mentor

Who provides mentoring and supervision?

Massage school instructors and continuing education providers have the opportunity to create ongoing supervision programs for their graduates.

Your employer, if she is an experienced massage therapist or health care practitioner, may also be available as a mentor or supervisor. In addition, some massage therapists ask a mental health professional or experienced massage therapist in their community to act in this capacity.

How do you ask someone to be your mentor or supervisor?

Seek out experienced therapists. Get bodywork from them; find out what they studied. Ask them for their personal story, take them out to lunch.

With some assertiveness and persistence, you will be able to find experienced bodyworkers willing to spend time with you -- especially if you approach them professionally and in a non- demanding way. The biggest reward -- other than lunch -- is for them to hear how you have used the knowledge they shared. After your first meeting, write a thank you note. This makes a good impression on your prospective mentor.

Suggested Qualifications for Massage Therapy Mentors and Clinical Supervisors

In order to be an effective mentor or supervisor, the following qualifications are recommended.

Work experience
A minimum equivalent to five years of full-time bodywork practice. (Full-time = 20 client contact hours per week.)

Rationale: This ensures the supervisor will have several years of experiential data to draw from. In other words, he is more likely to have experienced and resolved numerous clinical issues, and knows what it is like to be a full-time massage therapist. I believe massage therapists who meet this criteria are more likely to appreciate the developmental process of becoming a massage therapist. They are more likely to have compassion for the protege instead of having only an academic understanding of the process.

Education
A. A massage therapy certification and/or license as required by the state he or she practices in.

B. Completion of at least one certification program in a massage therapy modality, e.g. structural bodywork, polarity, neuromuscular, myofascial release.

C. Completion of at least one experientially based educational program (minimum 12 hours) in counseling skills, supervision, mediation, or communication.

Rationale: This ensures the supervisor will have: a) a massage therapy credential, b) at least one other theoretical framework to draw from in addition to Swedish massage, and c) some advanced communication and processing skills.

Supervision of supervisors

Massage therapists who work as mentors/supervisors should seek out their own regular peer support from other mentors. Whenever possible, include student assessments of your work in this process.

Rationale: The mentor is very likely to go through his or her own developmental process of acquiring and applying new skills. Mentoring has its own stresses, strains and ethical concerns that need to be supported and processed.

Mentoring and supervision scope of practice

The supervisory consultation is limited to addressing issues pertaining to the clinical application of massage therapy and ethical issues.

These are interventions and processes that will:
a) advance the clinical skills of a massage therapist

b) help develop his/her ethical sense, and

c) identify and help resolve any actual or perceived barriers or limitations that impair the supervisee's ability to practice massage therapy. It is the supervisor's responsibility to know the limits of his or her skills and to refer the supervisee to another professional when necessary.

Suggested Code of Ethics for Mentoring and Clinical Supervision in the Massage Therapy Profession

---

The mentor or supervisor:

1. Has explored his or her values, expectations and motivations as a massage therapist, as a mentor/supervisor, and as an individual.

2. Understands the roles, functions, goals and expectations of mentoring and supervision and explains them to the protege.

3. Understands the context in which he/she performs these roles.

4. Helps explore the professional and personal values, expectations, goals and motivations of the protege.

5. Understands the issues that often arise in each of the preceding four.
   a. Understands that mentoring and supervision is an unequal relationship.

b. Avoids dual relationships with the protege, especially sexual relationships.
c. Maintains confidentiality and explains the scope of confidentiality.
d. Evaluates the protege by mutually agreed-upon criteria and procedures.
e. Accurately represents his/her education, training and experience.
f. Is sensitive to differences regarding age, gender, socioeconomic status, sexual orientation, religious and ethnic backgrounds.
g. Refrains from any activity in which personal problems are likely to lead to inadequate service or harm to the protege.

6. Knows the code of ethics and legal statutes pertaining to the massage therapy profession.

7. Carries adequate liability insurance and ensures that his proteges do, too.

Common Roles and Responsibilities of Supervisors

Supervisors can play a variety of roles, each of which has its unique responsibilities. For example:

Scenario 1
Role: Supervisor is an instructor in a massage school or continuing education program

Responsibility: To students, massage school owner, education director, and future clients

Scenario 2
Role: Supervisor is an elected or appointed officer (committee chair) in a professional association, supervising committee members and committee projects

Responsibility: To board of directors, committee members, and association members

Scenario 3
Role: Supervisor hired by supervisee for own professional development

Responsibility: To supervisee and her clients

Scenario 4
Role: Supervisor is an employer managing employees in a business or clinical setting

Responsibility: To customers, owners or shareholders, and employees

Scenario 5
Role: Supervisor is hired by employer to supervise employees

Responsibility: To customers, owners or shareholders, and employees

Scenario 6

Role: Supervisor is hired or appointed by the Board of Massage Therapy (or other state licensing agency), to supervise a massage therapist who is on probationary status, rehabilitating from a substance abuse problem, etc.

Responsibility:
To Board of Massage Therapy (or other state licensing agency), massage therapist, and her clients.

The Mentoring/Supervision Model

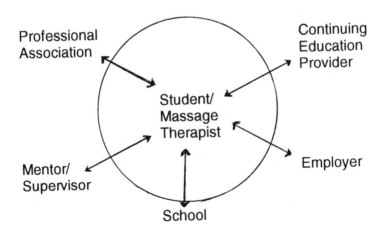

Characteristics of an Effective Mentor or Clinical Supervisor

In your search for mentors, look for someone who:

• Has made plenty of mistakes in his career, yet acknowledges them and has learned from them.

• Has compassion and patience versus righteousness, judgment, and shaming attitudes.

• Is willing to help you in your career development.

• Respects you and your process.

• Has sufficient experience and expertise in the field and knows the limits of his expertise.

• Maintains confidentiality.

• Guards against forming a dual relationship with you.

• Maintains her continuing education.

• Creates and maintains safety in the relationship.

• Communicates with integrity, owning his point of view instead of stating opinions as facts.

• Is a good listener.

• Lets you develop your own style.

- Is a well-regarded professional in your community.

- Is a person with whom you can relax and laugh.

- Has the self-confidence and wisdom to know when to let you move on.

What are warning signs of poor mentors and clinical supervisors?

They state opinions as facts and believe there is only one way to do things. In other words, they see the world in black and white terms.

What additional points should you consider when starting a mentoring or supervisory relationship?

The supervisor's training, theoretical and philosophical orientation will greatly influence the feedback he/she will give.

I believe the protege is much more empowered by a *discovery process* than a *guru approach*. The difference between these two is:

The discovery process	*The "guru" approach*
• unique path for protege	• clone of the mentor
• gradual positive long-term learning	• quick-fix learning style

41

- student has ability and power to solve his/her own problems

- mentor solves the protege's problems

- lower risk for projection/ transference

- high risk for projection/ transference

Even supervisors with the best intentions may cross the line between these two roles (perfection is impossible). This especially happens when the student wants to become a clone of the teacher or turn the mentor into a god or guru.

Chapter 4

The Motivated Mentee

What makes a good protege or supervisee?

The best supervisee has enough self-esteem and self-worth to ask for help. He also has the sincere motivation to help people and the willingness to develop personally and professionally. A good protege is willing to make and keep commitments.

How do you ask someone to be your mentor or supervisor?

Seek out experienced therapists. Get bodywork from them; find out what they studied. Ask them for their personal story, take them out to lunch.

With some assertiveness and persistence, you will be able to find experienced bodyworkers willing to spend time with you -- especially if you approach them professionally and in a non- demanding way. The biggest reward -- other than lunch -- is for them to hear how you have used the knowledge they shared. After your first meeting, write a thank you note. This makes a good impression on your prospective mentor.

What types of learning needs do mentees have?

Few mentors and supervisors can be experts in everything, so look for practitioners who have the specific talents and skills to assist you. It is not uncommon to have different mentors to serve different needs, for example:

Technical   **Evaluation skills**
Muscle testing
Palpation
Body reading, etc.

Conceptual   **Massage therapy theories, philosophies**
Deep tissue
Craniosacral
Shiatsu
Myofascial release, etc.

Technical   **Massage therapy hands-on techniques**
Deep tissue
Craniosacral
Shiatsu
Myofascial release, etc.

Technical   **Clinical applications**
Low back pain
TMJ
Whiplash
Carpal tunnel syndrome
Headaches, etc.

Technical   **Business**
Marketing
Planning

	Operating procedures
	Insurance billing and collection
Process	**Relationship issues**
	Client-therapist relationships
	Professional relationships
	Personal relationships
Process	**Intrapersonal**
	Support for personal growth and change
	Support for confronting feelings
	Support in re-evaluating fears, values, attitudes, belief systems

How often should you receive supervision?

While the frequency and amount of supervision needed varies from one therapist to another, some guidelines do apply. For new massage therapists with fewer than four years of full-time work experience, I recommend two hours of individual or group mentoring/supervision per 15 treatment hours. I recommend this for the first four years of practice. In other words, a massage therapist with three years experience who treats clients for 30 hours a month should seek out four hours of mentoring a month. A full-time massage therapist is defined as one who provides 20 hours of direct client care per week.

Chapter 5

The Mentoring Process

What clinical massage therapy issues are addressed in mentoring and clinical supervision ?

The following issues are frequently handled by mentors and supervisors in their work with their students:

• Application of assessment and evaluation skills

• Application of massage therapy techniques to various conditions

• Treatment plans protocols

• Tracking the therapeutic process (client process and progress)

• Ethical dilemmas

• Client-therapist relationship issues

• Communication issues

• Knowing when to refer a client or terminate treatment

• Commitment issues

• Fears and considerations that keep therapists from taking risks

• Effects of the massage therapist's personal life on his ability to practice

• Referring clients to other appropriate professionals for assistance

• Emotional release and trauma issues

Note that practice-building and business issues are considered mentoring concerns, and are not addressed in a supervisory relationship.

Therapeutic and interpersonal issues, however, are handled by a supervisor.

During the initial session, the mentor and her protege will identify and discuss the *short-term and long-term goals, expectations and learning objectives* of both protege and mentor, including:

- How frequently to meet
- Length of relationship
- Length of session(s)
- Evaluation process and criteria (if any)
- How to terminate the relationship (if necessary)
- Fees (if any). If sessions are free, be sensitive to your mentor's time and other commitments. Keep concerns short and focused.
- Goals for the session.

Once the relationship is established, do whatever will accomplish the goals (e.g. discussion, role-play, observation). Be as creative as you want.

Case example: A massage therapist brings her client (or a model) to massage in the presence of the mentor in order to receive feedback on applying specific techniques she recently learned. She took a class on the techniques four weeks ago but still does not feel confident with it.

Protege:
> 1.Brief the client on the purpose of the session.
>
> 2. Establish the necessary boundaries.

Mentor:
> 1. Follow the steps established in the initial session.
>
> 2. Summarize the main points of the techniques, the theory behind them and indications and contra-indications (if any).
>
> 3. Demonstrate how to evaluate the client.
>
> 4. Demonstrate the techniques (either partially or completely) and ask the client to pay attention to the sensation of receiving the technique. This allows her to give feedback to the protege.
>
> 5. Ask protege if she has any questions and answer them.

6. Have protege demonstrate the technique on the client.

7. Offer feedback and coaching as needed.

8. Debrief on the experience, paying attention to what worked and felt right, and what did not. Include client in the debriefing, as appropriate. If necessary, repeat any of the above steps.

9. Suggest tasks for homework to reinforce the experience or skills learned.

10. Schedule another session for follow-up or to address other issues.

11. Close.

After the session, both the mentor and protege should follow up on the experience.

Protege:
1. Act on the advice, experience and information given.

2. Provide status reports to the mentor relating to how you are using what you learned.

3. Express your appreciation for your mentor's time and talents, either verbally or in writing. This is considered professional.

Mentor:
1. Reflect on and self-evaluate teaching skills.

A suggestion to mentors and supervisors

Since different therapists begin from different baselines of competence and experience when starting the mentoring process, the mentor should work towards one of the following goals for each protege:

a) develop a bodyworker from novice to competent professional
b) develop a competent professional to an expert, or
c) develop an expert into a mentor or supervisor for the next generation of therapists.

Chapter 6

More Methods for Learning and Receiving Support

What additional opportunities are there for massage therapists to observe, learn and work in professional situations?

Additional ways to receive guidance and support fall into two categories: job-based and peer-based.

What are examples of job-based support systems?

Internships - These involve an academic institution, the sponsoring agency, and interns. Thus, the planning and assessing of goals and expectations among these three entities requires much communication and coordination.

These may be paid or voluntary positions for which you may receive school or continuing education credit. They can be set up as part-time or full-time commitments, ranging from a few months to a year.

Examples of sponsoring agencies are hospitals, clinics, collegiate and professional athletic training rooms.

Currently in Florida, the Central Florida School of Massage, Space Coast Massage Institute and Woods Hygienic Institute have internship programs for their massage therapy students.

I believe the need for quality supervision will increase dramatically as more schools and continuing education programs establish postgraduate internship programs.

Practicums and field study - These are typically the same as internships, except that they involve a shorter time commitment on the part of the intern.

Residencies - Again, these are much like internships, except that they involve a longer time commitment by the resident. Sponsoring agencies are usually hospitals and clinics.

Externships and independent study - These usually involve specific tasks and requirements for the completion of an educational experience leading towards a certification.

What are examples of peer-based support systems?

Peer consultation (one-on-one) - Consulting with another professional (who is an equal in level of training and work experience), to share information and provide mutual guidance and support. This can take place in a structured or unstructured format.

Peer consultation groups, support groups or study groups – These are opportunities to share information and network with other massage therapists; provide mutual guidance and support as equals; and review and practice specific skills. These groups can be facilitated by a mentor, and be structured or unstructured.

Such groups may be formally sponsored or coordinated through massage therapy schools, professional association chapter meetings, continuing education programs or massage therapy clinics.

They can also be informally coordinated much like one group in Gainesville, Florida which meets for breakfast monthly.

The idea of peer support groups is still relatively new to our field. To facilitate starting your own group, a few pointers are given below:

Guidelines for Running a Peer, Support or Study Group

Decide on the following points:

Group structure - *Open group* - new members can join any time. *Closed group* - does not admit new members; this allows for more trust.

Decision-making process - I recommend group consensus versus a majority rule.

Group size - Less than ten is recommended to encourage deeper sharing and greater participation.

Commitment - Is this an open group (people come and go) or closed group (with agreement to attend every meeting)?

Length of meeting - This depends on the group size, goals and purpose of the group.

Frequency and location - This again depends on the goals and purpose of the group.

Discussion and activities - These can range from pre-determined topics and activities to addressing whatever is present for the group members. (See *Appendix* for group activities.)

Addition of new members - Dedicate part of the meeting to integrating a new member, sharing a brief history and intentions.

Goals and purpose of the group - The focus can range from clinical practice issues and business issues to personal empowerment issues. (See *What clinical massage therapy issues are addressed in mentoring and supervision?* page 47)

Leadership issues - Effective groups have strong leaders who will commit to taking responsibility for managing the details. I believe leadership and responsibility needs to be shared among group members.

Although each member is personally responsible for contributing to the safety of the group, decide by whom and how the group will be facilitated (opening, maintaining order, safety and closing). Also decide when and how leadership will rotate. (See *Suggested qualifications for massage therapy mentors and clinical supervisors,* page 34.)

Ground rules

1. No personal attacks or blaming. Own your feelings.
2. Use active listening. Listen from your heart.
3. Make an effort to understand others.
4. Be open-minded. This goes both ways.
5. Let people finish. Don't interrupt.
6. Use personal experiences and "I" statements. Speak from your heart.
7. Try not to stereotype.
8. Avoid belaboring a point.
9. Validate and affirm each other.
10. Stay as present as possible.

Document the agreed-upon group structure, ground rules and leadership decisions and distribute copies to members.

Group process

Opening - Start with a saying, prayer, reading, exercise etc. that heightens the group focus to the here and now (grounding).

Middle - This is open to the group's creativity, personal needs and talents.

Closing - Summarize the experience and express gratitude to the group for its connection and support.

Chapter 7

Lessons from Geese

As each goose flaps its wings, it creates an "uplift" for the bird following. By flying in a V-formation, the whole flock adds seventy-one percent more flying range than if each bird flew alone.

Lesson: People who share a common direction and sense of community can get where they are going quicker and easier because they are travelling in the thrust of one another.

Whenever a goose falls out of formation, it suddenly feels the drag and resistance of trying to fly alone and quickly gets back in formation to take advantage of the "lifting" power of the bird immediately in front.

Lesson: If we have as much sense as a goose, we will stay in formation with those who are headed where we want to go.

When the lead goose gets tired, it rotates back into formation and another goose flies at the point position.

Lesson: It pays to take turns doing the hard tasks and sharing leadership with people, as with geese interdependent with each other.

The geese in formation honk from behind to encourage those up front to keep up their speed.

Lesson: We need to make sure that our honking from behind is encouraging and not something less helpful.

When a goose gets sick or wounded or shot down, two geese drop out of formation and follow it down to help and protect it. They stay with the goose until it is either able to fly again or dies. Then they will launch out on their own with another formation or catch up with their own formation.

Lesson: If we have as much sense as geese, we will stand by each other as they do.

-- Anonymous

Chapter 8

Post-Graduate Training

Our clinical massage therapy skills are at the core of who we are as a profession. In effect, they are what we do with our hands.

Most massage therapists are motivated to seek out more training for one or more of the following reasons. They need a confidence booster, in other words, they lack confidence in their skills to work with the types of clients showing up on their tables. They may also feel stuck or isolated, which affects their ability to be as effective with their clients as they would like. Other therapists seeking out training want to take their career to another level and grow as a professional. Finally, some bodyworkers need to meet licensing requirements for continuing education or simply want to learn something new.

In order to meet their needs, many bodyworkers will invest much time and money in an infusion (or transfusion) of new information and experience. It is not unusual for new massage therapists to invest several thousands of dollars and hundreds of hours in training, during their first three years of practice alone!

Some therapists never get beyond an introduction to a large variety of modalities, while others choose to pursue in-depth training in one or more modalities.

The core of advanced massage therapy training is based on weekend workshops. Some of these lead to certifications. Continuing education units are usually included, in order to meet licensing and national certification requirements.

These trainings and certifications sometimes require an intensive commitment of time and money on the part of the bodyworker. In addition, the burden is on the massage therapist to assess and evaluate which workshop will result in the biggest return on their investment (e.g. financial gains, increased confidence, long-term usefulness, and applicability of skills learned).

> *The gift of touching people's lives*
> *is too precious to take for granted.*

What modalities are available?

I believe learning at least one modality in each category will prepare you to work with a variety of injury and pain conditions. This model promotes mastery of knowledge and skills, and diversity of education. These modalities are categorized as:

Structurally-based myofascial restructuring methods (e.g. Core Bodywork, Structural Energetic Therapy, Rolfing™, Postural Integration).

Craniosacral work methods (e.g. Dr. John Upledger's method, Dr. Dallas Hancock's NICS method, Dr. Michael Shea's work).

Energetic bodywork methods (e.g. Polarity Therapy, Healing Touch, Jin Shin Do™, Acupressure).

Neuromuscular therapy methods (e.g. Judith Walker-Delany's method, Paul St. John's method, Dr. Leon Chaitow's method, Dr. Michael Vidal's method).

Flexibility methods (e.g. Aaron Mattes - Active-Isolated Stretching, Yoga).

Movement re-education methods (e.g. Feldenkrais, Alexander Technique, Pilates Reformer).

Colon hydrotherapy is a very effective modality for general and specific health improvement. Bodyworkers who have not received training in this modality should establish referral relationships with colonhydrotherapists in their communities.

Also recommended are courses in the following:

- *Risk management and ethics*
- *Insurance billing*
- *SOAP charting*
- *Medical terminology*
- *Communication skills*

- Rehabilitation process
- Nutrition and supplements in tissue healing

and on-going peer consultation or supervision.

What are the components of training programs?
Most modality training programs have the following components:

Theory and philosophy - the framework that guides the bodyworker's clinical thinking and decision-making process.

Anatomy and physiology - a review of pertinent anatomy and physiology.

Methodology - answers the when, where, why and how of the clinical application of techniques.

Evaluation / assessment techniques - are dependent on methodology. They combine interviewing and hands-on techniques (palpation skills) for data collection to determine indications, contraindications and the nature of the problem.

Treatment techniques - the actual hands-on skills (e.g. skin rolling, cross fiber friction).

The evaluation procedures and treatment techniques used often depend on the modality practiced. For example, a Shiatsu therapist will have a different set of evaluation skills and techniques than a Myofascial Release or Polarity therapist.

Without a methodology or therapeutic framework to guide your evaluation and treatment, you are, in a sense, guessing or operating on pure intuition. This can be dangerous and unethical when you are working with clients who are injured or in pain.

How do you clarify which modality to pursue?

Ask yourself:
- What are your personal interests and aptitude for learning a specific modality?

- Have you experienced the modality or treatment method first-hand, preferably for several sessions and by an experienced practitioner of that modality?

- Did you get the results and experience that you expected or were told to expect?

- What are the practitioner's opinions of and experience with the training program?

- What kind of people do you want to help with massage?

- Do you have the temperament, patience and emotional clarity to work with the client populations for which the modality is designed (e.g. persons dealing with physical and emotional pain, infants, the elderly, athletes, persons with AIDS)?

- Is the training available in your area, or will it require you to travel?

- Do you have the resources to afford it now, or do you need to plan on how to pay for it?

National, state and regional massage therapy conventions or conferences are a cost-effective way to get an introduction to various modalities from many of the profession's top educators. You will get a sampling of instructors' styles, while learning new theories and techniques.

I strongly recommend that once you find a modality you like, you learn it deeply. Immerse and ground yourself in it until you become an expert. Then pick up the next modality and hone your expertise in that, too. Repeat this cycle until you have *at least* three solid modalities in your professional arsenal.

Once you have completed the training, ask yourself:

- Do you feel competent in applying the skills you learned to working with your clients?

- If not, what do you need to do feel competent or develop your skills?

- Do you feel confident in educating your clients (and prospective clients) about the theory, methodology and treatment methods you have learned?

- If not, what do you need to do to feel confident and articulate what you know?

"Practice, practice, practice" or "See one, do one, teach one"?

Most educators and trainers understand that the assimilation of new information involves a learning curve. Students may take weeks or months to feel confident and demonstrate competence. For adults this learning curve can be significantly reduced when information is presented in manageable units or skills and reinforced often.

Since most bodywork training is experiential, the process of learning and experiencing new skills often brings up emotional, psychological and spiritual issues for the student. This experience can be very healing. However, even a student who is intellectually and physically able to learn and perform these new skills, may have a challenge practicing and integrating them if she is dealing with core issues of abandonment, shame or low self-esteem brought up by the training.

For this reason, the more progressive bodywork post-graduate programs help shorten the learning curve by encouraging practice. They have their students form and attend study groups and seek out experienced practitioners in their area, while at the same time providing support services to deepen and reinforce the newly acquired skills.

On the other hand, the mentoring and peer consultation process covered in Part One is also a way to shorten the learning curve and greatly enhance your educational experience. The process provides a powerful environment in which to practice specific techniques or skills you have learned, receive feedback and share with peers.

So how do we answer the question, "practice, practice, practice" or "see one, do one, teach one"? If you want the maximum benefit from a training, you need not only reinforcement but also continued support from your peers. In other words, although either approach is effective, neither one alone is enough for mastery and competence; we need both.

Chapter 9

Professional Identity

What kind of massage therapist do you want to be?

Do you want to co-create with your clients, or trust others to make decisions for you?

An aide just follows the physician's orders or his client's requests. For example, a physician may issue a prescription for "massage 15 min. 3x wk to cervical region."

Or a client may walk in and request "a half-hour massage for my lower back; I hurt it three months ago and it really bothers me."

In other words, when you act as an aide, you assume the physician or client knows your job better than you do.

A therapist, by contrast, feels empowered to make and modify treatment decisions based on her clinical training. A therapist does not simply follow the physician's orders or client's requests.

To further illustrate this contrast between an aide and a therapist, consider the following scenarios:

(1) A client brings in a prescription for "massage 15 min. 3x wk to cervical region." Instead of giving her this short

session right away, you evaluate the client, then ask for a new prescription from the physician based on what you have found:

"Considering the client's symptoms and evaluation, treatment goals include: inflammation and pain reduction, postural improvement and increased range of motion. Expected results in 10 to 13 weeks. I believe this can be achieved with 90-minute sessions of deep tissue massage therapy to cervical, shoulder, upper back and chest regions, 2x per wk for 2-3 wks to address inflammation, ischemia and trigger points; then 1x per wk for 2-3 wks to address structural alignment; then space sessions 10, 12, and 15 days apart as structural alignment improves, addressing restrictions to range of motion by releasing adhesions and scar tissue."

(2) A client comes in asking for a half-hour massage for his back pain. Instead of giving him what he asks for, you respond "I understand you want a half-hour massage for your lower back pain. Are you only interested in temporary relief, or are you also interested in healing the injured muscles and resolving this pain syndrome?" (See *Chapter 10: The Therapeutic Relationship* for more on client interviewing techniques.)

In both scenarios, the bodyworker is a therapist, not an aide. As such, he is a competent professional and his own input and feedback is necessary (even vital) for the effective treatment of the client.

A dilemma in our profession is that many therapists do not understand the distinction between the role of an aide and that of a therapist. This raises several ethical concerns when we are working with clients who are injured or in pain and subsequently billing insurance for our services. (See *Chapter 11: The First Client Session.*)

Is your professional identity modality-based or profession-based?

In Florida (and many other states), massage therapy had a poor public image until recently. It was often associated with adult entertainment (e.g. massage parlors, escort services, prostitution) and other more benign attitudes (e.g. "It can't possibly be therapeutic for pain relief," "Only flakes do massage," and "It's not a valuable service"). The reaction to this lack of credibility of the profession was that many practitioners made efforts to distance themselves from identifying themselves as massage therapists. They called themselves neuromuscular therapists, deep tissue therapists, bodyworkers, etc., instead. This protected them from the image associated with massage therapy. It often gave them an exotic uniqueness and a marketing strategy (in addition to specialization and advanced skills).

However, this trend had a dark side. The profession's credibility eventually improved, and public awareness and acceptance of massage therapy increased. But at the same time, the stigma toward therapists who practiced only relaxation massage and did not self-identify with a modality grew within the profession itself. It was no longer considered enough to be "just" a relaxation massage therapist. Conversely, therapists who did not have a clinical orientation in their training and practice judged those who did as being too medically or allopathically oriented.

This elitist attitude has been problematic and divisive for the profession. Health care practitioners can be judgmental and closed-minded toward each other -- I have seen this even in myself. Prejudices are usually expressed in confidence, but are still harmful to the profession. They include:

"Neuromuscular therapists are more competent than massage therapists who only do relaxation work or Swedish massage."

"Deep tissue work is too invasive and should be avoided. Cranial work is less invasive and a lot more effective."

"Cranial work is too subtle to effect any significant change."

"Clients should never feel pain during massage treatments."

"Modality X is the right (or only) way to do (treat) symptom Y."

These attitudes are usually due to ignorance, insecurity and personal agendas. I believe this is part of the reason why massage therapists do not discuss clinical cases with each other as often as they need to for professional and personal well-being.

We need to recognize how much we need our peers for support and how useless elitism within the profession is. This healing within the profession will make both the massage therapists and the profession stronger and more effective. The groundwork for mentoring and supervision needs to be laid now.

Chapter 10

The Therapeutic Relationship

One role of mentors and supervisors is to help therapists refine their technical skills. Another should be to empower them in their client-therapist relationships. This second role is usually overlooked by other books on mentoring; however, it is essential in developing an effective and professional connection with individuals who entrust us with their pain.

An additional reason for including this discussion in a book on mentoring is that the concepts covered here also apply to the therapeutic relationship between the *mentor* and *mentee*.

When we choose to do clinical massage therapy with clients healing from injuries, chronic pain and emotional trauma, we need to be conscious of the clients' emotional state and psychological reference points, not only their physical bodies. Therefore, it is necessary to take *Universal Precautions* with the therapeutic relationship.

Massage therapists need to clarify clients' expectations during the first session, educate them fully about the therapist's abilities and limitations, and develop achievable goals. This ensures that clients recover faster, and are more committed to completing prescribed therapy and rehabilitation goals. As a result, the therapist will be perceived as a competent professional who cares about his client.

It is important that you:

• Initiate sufficient client interaction to establish therapeutic boundaries, identify the nature of the problem, and determine client goals and course of treatment.

• Empower the client to accept responsibility for his/her decisions and agreements in her health care.

• Provide client education to help her recognize that recovery from pain and injury often requires some lifestyle changes, especially for future prevention and wellness.

• Treat the client as a whole, recognizing the physical, mental/emotional, spiritual, social and environmental aspects of the individual.

How do clients respond to pain or trauma?

Each individual's response to pain and trauma is unique. However, there are certain identifiable patterns:

Perception of pain - Some clients become desensitized to their bodies and even report they are not in pain, while others become hypersensitive and know where every ache is.

Disclosure of information - Some talk freely about themselves and their problems (sometimes too much); others feel very uncomfortable talking about their problems.

Sense of boundaries - Clients on one end of the continuum have skewed personal boundaries; they are unable to speak up or assert themselves to set limits. Clients at the other extreme may become hypersensitive to personal boundaries and feel distrustful, defensive and scared.

Clients often have old unresolved physical or emotional traumas underlying the current injury or trauma.

Therefore, we need to model healthy boundaries not only for the clients' safety and personal growth, but also to maximize the positive effect of the bodywork on their healing process. When healthy boundaries are not established with such clients, the predictable end result is low commitment and energy investment in the therapeutic process and necessary life style changes.

It is important to brief clients on what may happen in their healing process, so they do not feel anxious or scared about what they do experience. This is important because you never know for sure what a client's history is.

I have found that even when clients fill out the intake form, approximately forty percent of their significant issues and history are not included. This omission may be because clients truly do not recall at the time, they do not want to reveal it or unconsciously choose not to remember. Nor are clients likely to fill in the missing parts of their history during a few sessions. Therefore, you can safely assume that the information on the intake form is somewhat incomplete or inaccurate.

Why are professional boundaries and client readiness important?

A client may not be ready for massage therapy if she is indecisive about what she wants or defers to a higher authority for decisions (e.g. a spouse, physician, or sister) and raises objections to getting a massage (e.g. lack of money, time).

As massage therapists we need to address such objections up-front. We cannot help anyone unwilling or incapable of making decisions and taking responsibility for himself. These individuals may be afraid, not interested in getting better, confused about their priorities, or not have enough information to make a decision. Whatever the reason, you can avoid a lot of headaches by dealing with objections up front.

Two types of clients in particular can be difficult to work with. The *doctor hopper* is looking for the quick fix and can not commit to a therapeutic process. The *overly dependent client* makes frequent phone calls, and needs support and reassurance, which can be very draining. This client is often an appropriate referral for professional psychological services (Dean & Barich, 1993).

I have found that when I establish clear boundaries up-front with such clients, they will either redirect themselves to more productive behavior or self-select out of treatment.

What are the four primary responsibilities and tasks of massage therapists?

Connecting - Relating and empathizing with clients through your presence. This means having the skills and ability to fully hear and respond appropriately to clients.

Creating safety - Setting and maintaining boundaries, collecting and providing sufficient and appropriate information where informed consent is established. Both client and therapist agree on and know the why, when, where, what and how of the work together.

Educating - Building body and self-awareness through experiential work and verbal explanation.

Empowering - Providing sufficient and appropriate validation, encouragement and support in the healing process.

What are the distinctions between listening and communication?

The massage therapist's self-awareness and communication skills are necessary tools in serving clients. Understanding the following distinctions and checking out what clients mean by certain words or phrases can help clarify the messages sent and received.

During an interview we need to attend to the following:

External information - The who, what when, where and why of the client's injury or accident.

Internal cognitive information (frame of reference) - Thoughts, beliefs, judgements, assumptions, opinions, perceptions, interpretations, values, attitudes, and expectations (unexpressed) of the client.

Internal kinesthetic information - The client's experience in his/her body, including emotions (e.g. fear, sadness, anger, joy, shame) and sensations (e.g. burning, aching, throbbing).

Process of communication - *verbal*: Use of vague vs. specific language to describe an experience; leaving out vs. including pertinent details; changing the topic to avoid answering a question vs. freely sharing information, etc.

Non-verbal/behavioral: Posture, gestures and facial expressions (e.g. looking away a lot, grimacing).

Motives - Desires, purpose, goals, wishes, needs, and expectations (expressed) of treatment.

When should you ask open versus closed questions?

During the client intake interview, ask both open and closed questions.

Open-ended questions let the client do the talking and provide you with information she feels is appropriate and you may not have thought to ask for. Such questions encourage sharing of thoughts and feelings:

- What activities have been difficult or painful since your injury?
- How are you feeling?
- Would you explain that a little more?
- Is there anything else I need to know before we get started?

Close-ended questions elicit either a yes or no response. They give you specific information, clarify a situation, direct the client to a decision, set a boundary or move her along (if she is telling long stories):

- Do you want to come in again next Tuesday?
- Have you been in an auto accident before this one?
- Where do you feel pain?

Deep listening is an act of kindness not only to the other person but also to ourselves.

What tools do you use in active listening?

Restating/Rephrasing - A restatement is an exact repetition or parroting of a client's words. Rephrasing is an attempt to say the same thing in your own words. (*Caution:* do not add your own interpretation or change the meaning of the client's communication.)

Summarizing - Paraphrasing and focusing what has been conveyed.

Encouraging - A non-directive response to keep the client talking: "I see," "Go on," or "Could you tell me more about that?"

Mirroring - Similar to a restatement. However, it focuses on attitudes, feelings and non-verbal expression to convey empathy (e.g. sadness, discouragement, pain).

When communicating with clients use clear, specific, concrete language. Avoid vague language.

Client education - Inform client that education is part of the treatment plan. Get her agreement to provide education when it is appropriate. Avoid lecturing or preaching to clients.

What psychological barriers may come up?

In order to establish and maintain effective and productive working relationships with clients, it is imperative that the massage practitioner understand the psychological dynamics of a therapeutic relationship.

Projection - "The mechanism by which a person attributes an unwanted emotion or characteristic to someone else in an effort to deny the emotion or characteristic as part of one's self" (Gladding, 1988, p. 56).

Shadow - "An unconscious part of the personality characterized by traits and attitudes, whether negative or positive, which the [person] tends to reject or ignore" (McNeely, 1987, p. 116).

Transference - "The repetition of past relationships with significant others such that these earlier feelings, behaviors and attitudes are 'transferred' or projected onto the therapist...thus, involves the misperception of the therapist by the client and may take many forms" (Brammer, Abrego & Shostrom, 1993, p. 200).

Countertransference - The therapist's reaction to a client, based on the therapist's past personal issues or in direct response to the client's feelings or behaviors; other reactions may be the therapist's own projection on the client (Timms and Connors, 1992).

At present, the ethical practice of massage therapy does not require massage therapists to remain alert to their countertransference, except in avoiding sexual behavior with clients.

There are eight ways in which countertransference may appear in a therapeutic relationship:

1. Being overprotective with clients manifests itself in an oversolicitous attitude.
2. Treating clients in benign ways may stem from the therapist's fears of the client's anger.
3. Rejection of clients may be based on perceiving them as needy and dependent.
4. The [massage therapist's] need for constant reinforcement and approval.
5. Seeing yourself in your clients [too much sympathy due to over-identifying with client's problem].

6. Sexual and romantic feelings between client and therapist.
7. Compulsive advice-giving.
8. Desire to develop social relationships with clients (Corey, Corey & Callnan, 1988, p. 50-53).

Asking yourself the following questions will help you the therapist prevent meeting your own needs at the expense of your clients':

-   What am I feeling as I am with this person?
-   What am I experiencing?
-   What do I want to say and do?
-   What am I aware of not saying to [or doing with] the client?
-   Do I find myself hoping the client will fail to show up?
-   Do I find myself wanting the client to stay longer?

(Corey et al., 1988, p. 50)

Dual relationships - A personal and/or business relationship with a massage therapy client that extends beyond the treatment room. Examples are friendships, romantic relationships or business partnerships.

There is much debate on whether dual relationships are ethical in the massage therapy profession. I believe the answer to the following questions will help you determine whether you can enter into a dual relationship with a client:

-   What are the therapeutic goals with your client?
-   Is the client currently pursuing litigation for his or her injury?
-   Is the client having transference responses to you?

- Are you having countertransference responses to your client?
- Is your therapeutic objectivity important to you and necessary to serve your client well?

Triangulation - "An unhealthy relationship among three people. Whenever a two-person relationship becomes unbearable, one or both of them may bring in a third person to help relieve their pain [stress]" (Whitfield, 1993, p. 159). This dynamic is also known as splitting behavior. In other words, when person A is unwilling (or unable) to confront person B directly regarding a problem, he tells a third person C (who also has a relationship with person B) about the gripe or problem. The intent is to get persons B and C into a conflict or to resolve the problem for A. This involves both overt and covert manipulation.

As massage therapists our primary professional relationship is with the client. However, we also have referral relationships with attorneys and physicians. Insurance companies are involved in client care especially when they pay the bills. Interacting with these entities usually works out well.

However, when communication breaks down between the client and his physician, attorney, or insurance company, you may be asked to intervene on behalf of the client or the physician or insurance carrier. This is most common with litigation cases and when therapists and physicians work together at a clinic. It can involve requests to pass along messages through you to another party. Even this can be very problematic, especially if the situation is emotionally charged. The therapist can get the brunt of an emotional outburst meant for someone else.

83

Triangulation

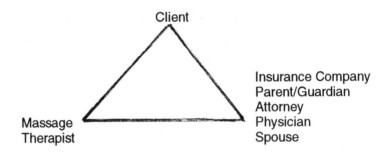

It is important to stay out of the triangulation as much as possible. Redirect the parties involved to talk to the appropriate person other than you. If the client refuses to do so or feels intimidated, direct him to the administrators or office managers of the parties involved.

Massage therapists are also capable of inadvertently creating triangles, so care must be taken to avoid such a situation. Therapists are at risk of rescuing others if they are not clear with their professional roles.

If you do intercede on the client's behalf, it is important to do so in an empowering versus disempowering manner.

Chapter 11

The First Client Session: Skills in Action

In the previous chapter you learned about the therapeutic relationship. In this chapter you will learn how to apply these skills in conducting the first client session. I will lay out six steps to follow, and discuss the purpose behind each. These steps provide a framework that the mentor can follow in monitoring the mentee's work, and goals to aim for in conducting the ideal first client session.

In order to build a strong therapeutic relationship and achieve the desired treatment goals, all six steps should be followed carefully.

It is important to allow at least thirty minutes for an initial interview with first-time clients.

What are the objectives of the first client session?

Objective 1:
Determine when, in relation to the onset of the injury or problem, the client is coming for help. Why is the client coming now? Why you or why massage therapy?

Objective 2:
Establish yourself as a professional. Build a connection and credibility with the client.

85

Objective 3:
Establish the client's commitment to his health and recovery. Get the client emotionally and physically involved in his healing process. Prepare the client for his journey. Brief him on what will happen.

Step 1: Intake Interview and History: Collecting data on the client

---

Purpose:
To identify variables or factors that may have or are contributing to the client's problem. Have the client talk about himself.

Intake forms:
- Scan the completed intake form
- Check for completeness, accuracy, client's awareness and truthfulness.
- Note who referred client (e.g. physician, other client).

History:
- Note work, hobbies, and sports activities.
- Check medical history.

Identify client's:
- Perceived/presenting problems, diagnoses, injuries and complaints (What is his problem and where does it hurt?)
- History of complaint (How long has he had the problem? Has this problem or something similar occurred before? What resolved it?)
- Complaint origins (When and how did the pain or

86

problem start?)

- Activities or movements affected by the injury or pain (e.g. getting dressed, typing, driving, sitting)
- Previous and current treatment effects: medications (addictions), surgical procedures, and other therapies.

Note obvious contraindications.

Note: Drug dependency on prescription medication often occurs with chronic pain clients. It is important to identify drug dependency early on, because it can sabotage your work. I inform chronic pain clients that my policy is to work with drug dependent clients only when they are actively involved in a drug treatment program.

Stress management:
- Has there been a change in sleep patterns, nutrition, libido, medication use, exercise, etc.?
- How does he feel about the pain (emotionally)?
- Move him from his head to his feelings!
- Identify emotional and psychological pain.
- What has the client lost and what does he hope to gain through treatment?
- Perceived effects and limitations: What is the personal cost to the client? Ask him to assign a value to the following losses:
  - income
  - time
  - strength
  - enjoyment
  - energy
  - status.

Premorbid coping response and compensation:
- How has client coped in the past?

Secondary gains (if any):
- What is the client avoiding or getting out of by being sick or hurting?

Cultural background:
- Note ethnicity, gender, age, sexual orientation, religion, socioeconomic level, education, or disability.
- Take into consideration cultural differences regarding healing and touch.

Summarize:
- Perceived/presenting problem.
- Reason for seeking treatment, motivation for healing.
- Impact of problem on client's life.

Step 2: Structuring the Session and the Relationship: Establishing relationship boundaries and getting informed consent

---

Purpose:
1. To set boundaries.
2. To communicate expectations.
3. To create safe container for therapy/healing to occur for both client and therapist.
4. Establish yourself as a professional.
5. Prepare the client for her journey.

The professional relationship and treatment are focused on the client's goals. Structure the relationship up-front (in person or on the phone).

Tell the client what to expect from you:

Tell her what you can or will do. Teach the client to be a client. Define and explain:

- The massage therapy process
  - rehabilitation process vs. medical model
  - methodology, theory and philosophy of modalities used
- Draping issues
  - bathing suit, underwear
  - towels, sheets
- Length of session
  - punctuality, policy for arriving late
- Fees and method of payment
  - deal with up-front, preferably on the phone
  - private pay or insurance verification
- Cancellation policies (due to client or therapist illness): Give the client a written copy of your policy. Medical facilities inform clients of their responsibility to call the office 24 hours in advance if they need to cancel their appointment (except for emergencies). Decide ahead of time whether or not you will charge a fee for less than 24-hour cancellation notice or no-shows (a client who did not keep a scheduled appointment).
- Confidentiality
  - What is discussed in the session remains confidential.
  - Use of treatment notes and reports for insurance companies and supervision.
  - Client remains anonymous during supervision and peer support meetings.

- Phone calls
  - Whether client can call you if he has any questions.
  - Note hours you can be reached.
  - Whether can you call client if you do not hear from him. If so, when and where?
- Your work hours.

Educate the client on what she may experience:

- Discuss your evaluation and client's history as it pertains to the problem or condition.
- Explain treatment and possible effects (during and after treatment).
  - May experience toxin release, emotional release, soreness, bruising. For example, persons with excessive adipose, weak tissues or adhesions are more likely to feel soreness and experience bruising.
  - Educate client on the use of ice, nutrients, water, etc., if bruising occurs.
  - Ask her to call you about any concerns.
- Identify any objections, considerations or beliefs about pain.
  - Explain what healthy relaxed tissue and injured tissue or tissue with chronic tension feels like (especially if client uses fear of pain as an objection).

I often explain pain in the following way. When applying slow deep pressure to a muscle (healthy relaxed tissue), the client should just feel pressure, no pain. If he feels pain with this pressure, then the tissue is not healthy and relaxed. In other words, it is injured, has adhesions, inflammation or atrophy. It may also be pumped up from exercise, emotional tension or stress. Pain indicates a problem. The pressure I apply is not causing the pain; it is already there.

This helps the client understand and take ownership for the sensations in his body. It is also useful to teach clients about the pain-stress cycle. The more information they have, the more likely they are to work through the pain.

Explain how to communicate pain:

Teach the client to express pain and discomfort directly. Tell the client that "it hurts" does not mean "stop" to the therapist; it is an expression of discomfort and feelings. Show the client that setting boundaries directly is best. A more direct way to tell the therapist that the pain is too intense to continue is to say "stop!"

Clarify what you expect from the client:

- Payment at time of service
- Providing insurance information
- Bringing prescriptions, etc.
- No sexual contact.
- Showing up for sessions.

Clarify what the client expects from you. Note initial goals and expectations:

- Relaxation, less pain, stress relief, better flexibility, etc.

- Find out their needs in relation to: activities, feelings and perception.

Step 3: Evaluation - A Systemic Approach:
Confirming presenting problems or identifying other issues

Purpose:
1. To help therapist identify problem(s) in order to create a treatment plan.
2. To increase client's awareness of his/her body and areas of discomfort and/or pain (symptoms).
3. To establish a base line of symptoms (before beginning treatment) and a baseline for documentation.
4. To provide the expected evaluation.
5. To show the client you are interested in him/her and want to find out what the problems are.
6. To identify when to refer to a physician, attorney or counselor.

Before performing an evaluation procedure, briefly explain to the client what you will do, how you will do it and what you expect to find out.

Evaluation Tools - used to increase client awareness and establish a baseline.

- *Physician's diagnosis* and/or client's presenting problem

- *Body reading* - structural alignment and compensation

- *Muscle testing* - to assess gross strength and compensation

- *Visual exam* of skin for open sores, bruises, etc.

92

- *Palpation exam* of soft tissue while attending to non-verbal and verbal cues. Identify:
  - trigger points, acupressure points, meridians, energy fields
  - hyper/hypotonicity, spasms, sensitivity to pressure
  - inflammation, fluid retention, ischemia
  - adhesions and scar tissue

- Active and passive *range of motion tests* and *manual resistive tests* - to identify and isolate injured tissues and determine range of motion.

Level of Physical Functioning - Activities of Daily Living
- Ask client to report what she could do before injury and what she can not do now.
- Whenever possible, have client demonstrate these movement restrictions and document the results. Isolate muscles and identify structural and energetic patterns.

Psychosocial Stressors
- Identify what is happening in the client's life with regard to stress.
- The intent is not to change her, but just to help her be aware of how it may affect her body. Educate the client.

Common Stressors:

- Accident or illness to self	- Wedding
- Accident or illness to family member	- Buying a house
- Death in the family	- Divorce
- Education or professional training	- Work

Note: *Physical and psychosocial stressors are usually inter-related.*

93

Documentation:
Note observations, palpation findings, and what the client reports.

Step 4: Treatment Plan and Client Education:
Co-creating treatment goals with the client

Purpose:
1. To lessen client resistance or fear through involvement.
2. To support client in committing to his healing process.
3. To tailor your services to his needs.
4. To establish goals for the session.
5. To outline short term goals.
6. To set long term goals (if necessary).
7. To fulfill insurance company requirement.
8. To keep you on track.
9. To help in re-evaluations. Ask, "Is there anything we missed? Do you feel complete?"

Review history, initial goals and evaluation
- Educate client on what you learned about his body, considering his activities, feelings and perception. Include:
    - evaluation tools used and body areas involved
    - levels of physical functioning
    - psychosocial stressors

- Check whether client's initial goals have changed, now that he is more aware.

Set short term treatment goals
- What to do for today's session.
- What to do (in the next two weeks or several weeks).

- Other health care practitioners you recommend the client sees.

Set long term treatment goals (if necessary)

Evaluate and educate on additional environmental and life style variables
- *Accessories:* purse on shoulder, wallet in back pocket, shoes (high heels), glasses
- *Consumption:* diet, nutritional supplements, detoxifying process
- *Ergonomics:* desk, chair, car seat, driving habits, bed, exercise.

Step 5: Treatment: Facilitating healing

Purpose: To help client recover and heal from pain and injury.

As bodyworkers, we provide massage therapy with our hands; listen and witness with our ears and eyes; and acknowledge, validate, bless, encourage, affirm and reinforce with our words, heart and presence.

Step 6: Closure and Follow-up: Ending the first session and proceeding with treatment plan.

Purpose: To monitor and continue the healing process.

Advise client on how to proceed after treatment to reinforce the positive effects of treatment and minimize set-backs:
- physical activity (e.g. Can he start playing tennis again after this treatment? Consider the example below.)
- self-care
- follow-up sessions with you
- follow-up sessions with primary care physicians.

Give the gift of awareness
- Follow client's process, how his/her function and symptoms improve over time.
- Advise that change and improvement does not always look like *the client expects.*
- Respond to the infamous phone call, "I'm not feeling any better."
- Help the client track and monitor his/her process and progress.
- Show him his progress when he is discouraged.
- Provide encouragement and reinforcement.

Validate changes (in relationships, work, health and other activities).
- Listen to changes in symptoms, which may mean progress and healing. State them as progress.

Case example: Help the client see how he may be sabotaging his progress. He reports that he had tennis elbow for three months and was unable to play tennis. Then he was pain-free after the first treatment, so he played two hours of tennis. If he comes in for the next session or calls complaining of pain again and tells you the therapy is not working, point out that he recovered enough to play tennis again. This may also be why he is hurting again.

Conclusion

L Like the hero on his quest, you the massage therapist have embarked on your healer's journey.

In this book, you have learned how to break the silence and reach out to other therapists for guidance, and how to find mentors and supervisors best matched to your goals and growth areas. The process of guiding fledgling healers in this professional journey can be equally rewarding for the mentor or supervisor. Our profession as a whole benefits from strong support systems.

Deciding what kind of therapist to be and which modalities to pursue is equally important for professional growth. In many cases it is no longer enough to have a massage therapy license or certification; knowing the theories and methodologies of several modalities can make you a more versatile and effective bodyworker.

Working with a client also involves communicating with the client. For this, an effective healer needs to understand the dynamics of the therapeutic relationship. While relationships with clients are complex and require careful structuring, they also carry the rewards of more effective communication, evaluation and treatment. Simply connecting with another human being in a more meaningful way is worth learning about setting boundaries and avoiding psychological games.

The model I have developed is meant as a road-map for dedicated bodyworkers to take on their journey. May it serve you in creating community among massage therapists in your area and deepen your effectiveness as a healer.

Prosperous journey!

Appendix

- The Six Competencies of the Massage and Bodywork Profession

- Suggested Group Activities, by Competency

- Sample Mentor Program Application

- Sample Protege Agreement

- The Six Steps of the First Client Session

- Sample Client History Form

- Professional Associations

These forms may be reproduced for your use in peer consultation groups, mentoring relationships and private practice. However, please include author acknowledgement and/or copyright information on any forms you reproduce.

The Six Competencies of the Massage and Bodywork Profession

1. **Self-Promotion:** The skills and ability to attract and generate new clients.

2. **Massage Therapy Skills and Professional Identity:** The hands-on technical knowledge and skills to effect positive change in our clients.

3. **Business Management:** The administrative knowledge and skills of running a business.

4. **The Therapeutic Relationship:** The human relationship skills to effect positive change in our clients. The application of professional ethics.

5. **Social Support:** Relationships and social activities that are recharging and supportive for the therapist.

6. **Personal Empowerment:** The knowledge, skills and experience to perceive one's self and behave in a manner that is life-affirming.

Suggested Peer Group Activities,
by Competency

---

1. Self-Promotion

Sales

˅ Demonstrate, practice and receive feedback on your phone skills.

˅ Demonstrate, practice and receive feedback on handling objections.

Marketing

˅ Develop brochures and promotional materials.

˅ Develop media advertising and share the cost.

˅ Develop and implement a marketing campaign in your community for massage therapy awareness month in November.

Public Speaking

˅ Demonstrate, practice and receive feedback on your public speaking skills.

˅ Encourage and support each other to speak to local clubs, associations, health food stores and bookstores on the benefits of massage therapy.

Writing

˅ Help each other write informative massage therapy articles for local newspapers and magazines.

Note: Whenever possible, coordinate your efforts with your local massage therapy association chapter.

2. Massage Therapy Skills and Professional Identity

˅ Share and receive the bodywork you need to maintain your body.

˅ Demonstrate, practice and receive feedback on new massage therapy skills you have learned.

˅ Demonstrate, practice and receive feedback on new assessment and evaluation skills you have learned.

˅ As a group hire a massage educator to teach or review certain skills.

˅ Discuss and practice SOAP charting.

˅ Discuss and receive feedback on actual SOAP notes, specifically on client progress and treatment strategies.

˅ Discuss theories, philosophies, and methodologies pertaining to selected modalities.

✔ Discuss the issues pertaining to specific health conditions (e.g. fibromyalgia).

3. Business Management

Organizing the Massage Therapist's Business

✔ As a group invite (or hire) a retired business executive to help you develop your business plan, mission, vision, and strategies. (Contact your local SCORE or SBDC.)

✔ Discuss the advantages and disadvantages of having an out-call business versus an office.

✔ As a group invite (or hire) an attorney to learn about incorporation versus sole proprietorship.

✔ Invite business support professionals such as lawyers, accountants, and insurance agents to learn how these professions can support your business.

Hiring, Training and Working with Staff

✔ Help each other create job descriptions and job responsibilities.

✔ Discuss advantages and disadvantages of hiring employees versus independent contractors.

✔ Discuss how to handle salaries, commissions, benefits and employment taxes.

©1998 Ernesto J. Fernandez

Scheduling and Maintaining Records

✔ Share how you use your insurance billing system.

✔ Share accounting strategies.

Managing the Money

✔ Learn to make budgets and reduce your overhead.

✔ Help each other with federal income tax and sales tax issues.

✔ Share strategies of your insurance collection system.

Time Management

✔ Share advice on scheduling clients, paperwork, etc.

4. The Therapeutic Relationship

✔ Demonstrate, practice and receive feedback on interviewing skills.

✔ Discuss ethical concerns you may have.

✔ As a group debrief issues that came up while working with your clients or referral sources.

✔ Demonstrate, practice and receive feedback on setting therapeutic boundaries.

©1998 Ernesto J. Fernandez

5. Social Support

˅ Discuss issues concerning you and your significant other (separations, divorces, recovering from an affair, etc.).

˅ Discuss issues concerning you and your family.

˅ Celebrate group birthdays and other significant events.

˅ Create and perform meaningful rituals for each other.

˅ Explore and practice re-creation activities.

6. Personal Empowerment

˅ Practice exercises to develop personal presence.

˅ Practice exercises to build self-esteem and positive body awareness.

˅ Practice setting personal boundaries.

˅ Discuss how your personal issues may be affecting your ability to work and meet your responsibilities.

˅ Discuss challenges with prosperity, and practice exercises to improve your prosperity.

˅ Meditate as a group.

˅ Discuss and support each other whenever health challenges arise.

˅ Discuss and explore gender, communication, spiritual and sexuality issues.

7. Group Activities That Can Be Applied to Any Competency

˅ Discuss books from the recommended reading list and other sources.

˅ Do visualization exercises.

˅ Practice role plays.

˅ In front of the group, make a personal commitment (e.g. to exercise every day or start counseling).

˅ Share your feelings, thoughts, desires and behaviors.

Sample Mentor Program Application

Please print or type your answers to the following questions on a separate sheet of paper. We expect frank and honest answers that reflect the thinking of a real person. We would be concerned if we got back answers that sounded too simplistic and pat. Brief, concise answers are fine. This application will also be shared with your mentor. Be sure to keep one copy for your records.

1. a) Occupation(s) prior to attending massage therapy school.

    b) What skills in your previous profession can transfer into massage therapy?

    c) Which massage school did you go to and when?

2. Are you a member of at least one national professional association? If yes, which one; if no, why not?

    Are you a member of your state professional association? If yes, which one; if no, why not?

3. Are you working as a massage therapist now?

    If yes, in what setting? How many sessions a week? If no, why not?

4. What indications of professionalism do you have in place (brochures, business phone, business cards, etc.)?

5. What types of massage therapy do you do or intend to do?

6. What advanced trainings have you completed?

    When, where, who instructed?

7. Have you ever had a mentor before?

8. What special strengths or skills do you have that we should know?

9. List some adjectives or phrases about yourself that would help us in our mentor/protege matching.

10. List some adjectives or phrases that would describe your ideal mentor.

11. What geographical areas of Florida would you consider convenient places to meet with your mentor?

12. Other comments or things we should know:

13. Would you be willing to commit yourself to attend all protege-focused meetings?

14. Why do you want to be a massage therapist? What motivates you?

15. To what extent is massage therapy a calling for you?

    Discuss massage therapy in terms of service to others.

16. What are your career goals, including but not limited to massage therapy?

17. Explain why you think the mentor program is a match for you and your needs.

18. *Willingness.* We expect proteges to be enthusiastic, willing, cooperative, and eager to support each other. To what extent and in what ways does this describe you in this program?

19. *Commitment.* Explain why you are committed enough to successfully complete this program.

20. *Competing Forces.* What demands or responsibilities do you have in your life that pull time and energy in a direction away from your commitment to this program? (Be realistic. This question is as much for you as it is for us.)

21. *Financial.* Describe your financial situation in terms of your ability to meet the financial requirements of the mentee program.

22. *Convention.* Will you attend your state or national convention? Discuss your plans.

23. *Schedule Conflicts.* Do you have any existing schedule conflicts that would prohibit your attendance at the mentor-protege meetings?

Sample Protege Agreement

Goals for _____

1. Attend all mentor-protege meetings.

2. Be an active member of a FSMTA chapter, committee or project.

3. Attend this year's FSMTA State Convention.

4. Be a member of a national professional association.

5. Create 10 referral sources.

6. Create and implement a business plan and marketing plan.

7. Complete a certification program in an advanced modality.

8. Design a brochure.

9. Receive massage once a week.

10. Learn therapeutic communication skills.

11. Learn insurance billing.

12. Learn and practice maintaining healthy boundaries.

13. Schedule and enjoy re-energizing quality time with family, friends and significant others.

I agree to accomplish the above goals by _____

Protege (Signed) _____

Mentor (Witness) (Signed) _____

Date _____

The Six Steps of the First Client Session

Use this outline on a clipboard to help guide you during the first interview.

Step 1: Intake Interview and History
Collecting data on the client

Purpose: To identify variables or factors that may have or are contributing to the client's problem. Have the client talk about himself.

Intake forms:
- Scan the completed intake form
- Check for completeness, accuracy, client's awareness and truthfulness.
- Note who referred client (e.g. physician, other client).

History:
- Note work, hobbies, and sports activities.
- Check medical history.

Identify client's:
- Perceived/presenting problems, diagnoses, injuries and complaints (What is his problem and where does it hurt?)

- History of complaint (How long has he had the problem? Has this problem or something similar occurred before? What resolved it?)

- Complaint origins (When and how did the pain or problem start?)

- Activities or movements affected by the injury or pain (e.g. getting dressed, typing, driving, sitting)

- Previous and current treatment effects: medications (addictions), surgical procedures, and other therapies.

©1998 Ernesto J. Fernandez

Note obvious contraindications.

Note: Drug dependency on prescription medication often occurs with chronic pain clients. It is important to identify drug dependency early on, because it can sabotage your work. I inform chronic pain clients that my policy is to work with drug dependent clients only when they are actively involved in a drug treatment program.

Stress management:
• Has there been a change in sleep patterns, nutrition, libido, medication use, exercise, etc.?

• How does he feel about the pain (emotionally)?

• Move him from his head to his feelings!

• Identify emotional and psychological pain.

• What has the client lost and what does he hope to gain through treatment?

• Perceived effects and limitations: What is the personal cost to the client? Ask him to assign a value to the following losses:
    - income   - enjoyment
    - time   - energy
    - strength   - status.

Premorbid coping response and compensation:
• How has client coped in the past?

Secondary gains (if any):
• What is the client avoiding or getting out of by being sick or hurting?

Cultural background:
• Note ethnicity, gender, age, sexual orientation, religion, socioeconomic level, education, or disability.

• Take into consideration cultural differences regarding healing and touch.

©1998 Ernesto J. Fernandez

Summarize:
- Perceived/presenting problem.
- Reason for seeking treatment, motivation for healing.
- Impact of problem on client's life.

Step 2: Structuring the Session and the Relationship
Establishing relationship boundaries and getting informed consent

Purpose:
1. *To set boundaries.*
2. *To communicate expectations.*
3. *To create safe container for therapy / healing to occur for both client and therapist.*
4. *Establish yourself as a professional.*
5. *Prepare the client for her journey.*

The professional relationship and treatment are focused on the client's goals. Structure the relationship up-front (in person or on the phone).

Tell the client what to expect from you:

Tell her what you can or will do. Teach the client to be a client. Define and explain:

- The massage therapy process
        - rehabilitation process vs. medical model
        - methodology, theory, philosophy, of modalities used

- Draping issues
        - bathing suit, underwear
        - towels, sheets

- Length of session
        - punctuality, policy for arriving late

©1998 Ernesto J. Fernandez

117

• Fees and method of payment
    - deal with up-front, preferably on the phone
    - private pay or insurance verification

• Cancellation policies (due to client or therapist illness)
Give the client a written copy of your policy. Medical facilities inform clients of their responsibility to call the office 24 hours in advance if they need to cancel their appointment (except for emergencies).

Decide ahead of time whether or not you will charge a fee for less than 24-hour cancellation notice or no-shows (a client who did not keep a scheduled appointment).

• Confidentiality
    - What is discussed in the session remains confidential.
    - Use of treatment notes and reports for insurance companies and supervision.
    - Client remains anonymous during supervision and peer support meetings.

• Phone calls
    - Whether client can call you if he has any questions.
    - Note hours you can be reached.
    - Whether can you call client if you do not hear from him. If so, when and where?

• Your work hours.

Educate the client on what she may experience:

• *Discuss your evaluation* and client's history as it pertains to the problem or condition.

• *Explain treatment and possible effects* (during and after treatment).
    - May experience toxin release, emotional release, soreness, bruising. For example, persons with excessive adipose, weak tissues or adhesions are more likely to feel soreness and experience bruising.

©1998 Ernesto J. Fernandez

118

- Educate client on the use of ice, nutrients, water, etc., if bruising occurs.
- Ask her to call you about any concerns.

• *Identify any objections,* considerations or beliefs about pain.
  - Explain what healthy relaxed tissue and injured tissue or tissue with chronic tension feels like (especially if client uses fear of pain as an objection).

Explain how to communicate pain:

Teach the client to express pain and discomfort directly. Tell the client that "it hurts" does not mean "stop" to the therapist; it is an expression of discomfort and feelings. Show the client that setting boundaries directly is best. A more direct way to tell the therapist that the pain is too intense to continue is to say "stop!"

Clarify what you expect from the client:

• Payment at time of service
• Providing insurance information
• Bringing prescriptions, etc.
• No sexual contact.
• Showing up for sessions.

Clarify what the client expects from you. Note initial goals and expectations:

• Relaxation, less pain, stress relief, better flexibility, etc.
• Find out their needs in relation to: activities, feelings and perception.

Step 3: Evaluation - A Systemic Approach
Confirming presenting problems or identifying other issues

Purpose:
1. To help identify problem(s) in order to create treatment plan.

©1998 Ernesto J. Fernandez

2. *To increase client's awareness of his / her body and areas of discomfort and / or pain (symptoms).*
3. *To establish a base line of symptoms (before beginning treatment) and a baseline for documentation.*
4. *To provide the expected evaluation.*
5. *To show the client you are interested in him / her and want to find out what the problems are.*
6. *To identify when to refer to a physician, attorney or counselor.*

Before performing an evaluation procedure, briefly explain to the client what you will do, how you will to do it and what you expect to find out.

Evaluation Tools - used to increase client awareness and establish a baseline.
• *Physician's diagnosis* and/or client's presenting problem

• *Body reading* - structural alignment and compensation

• *Muscle testing* - to assess gross strength and compensation

• *Visual exam* of skin for open sores, bruises, etc.

• *Palpation exam* of soft tissue while attending to non-verbal and verbal cues. Identify:
  - trigger points, acupressure points, meridians, energy fields
  - hyper/hypotonicity, spasms, sensitivity to pressure
  - inflammation, fluid retention, ischemia
  - adhesions and scar tissue

• Active and passive *range of motion tests* and *manual resistive tests*
  - To identify and isolate injured tissues and determine range of motion.

Level of Physical Functioning - Activities of Daily Living
• Ask client to report what she could do before injury and what she can not do now.

• Whenever possible, have client demonstrate these movement

restrictions and document the results. Isolate muscles and identify structural and energetic patterns.

Psychosocial Stressors
- Identify what is happening in the client's life with regard to stress.
- The intent is not to change her, but just to help her be aware of how it may affect her body. Educate the client.

Common Stressors:

- Accident or illness to self	- Wedding
- Accident or illness to family member	- Buying a house
- Death in the family	- Divorce
- Education or professional training	- Work

Physical and psychosocial stressors are usually interrelated.

Documentation:
Note observations, palpation findings, and what the client reports.

Step 4: Treatment Plan and Client Education
Co-creating treatment goals with the client

Purpose:
1. *To lessen client resistance or fear through involvement.*
2. *To support client in committing to his healing process.*
3. *To tailor your services to his needs.*
4. *To establish goals for the session.*
5. *To outline short term goals.*
6. *To set long term goals (if necessary).*
7. *To fulfill insurance company requirement.*
8. *To keep you on track.*
9. *To help in re-evaluations. Ask, "Is there anything we missed? Do you feel complete?"*

Review history, initial goals and evaluation
- Educate client on what you learned about his body, considering his

©1998 Ernesto J. Fernandez

activities, feelings and perception. Include:
- evaluation tools used and body areas involved
- levels of physical functioning
- psychosocial stressors

• Check whether client's initial goals have changed, now that he is more aware.

Set short term treatment goals
• What to do for today's session.
• What to do (in the next two weeks or several weeks).
• Other health care practitioners you recommend the client sees.

Set long term treatment goals (if necessary)

Evaluate and educate on additional environmental and life style variables:
• *Accessories:* purse on shoulder, wallet in back pocket, shoes (high heels), glasses
• *Consumption:* diet, nutritional supplements, detoxifying process
• *Ergonomics:* desk, chair, car seat, driving habits, bed, exercise.

Step 5: Treatment:
Facilitating healing

Purpose: To help client recover and heal from pain and injury.

As bodyworkers, we provide massage therapy with our hands; listen and witness with our ears and eyes; and acknowledge, validate, bless, encourage, affirm and reinforce with our words, heart and presence.

Step 6: Closure and Follow-up
Ending the first session and proceeding with treatment plan.

Purpose: To monitor and continue the healing process.

Advise client on how to proceed after treatment to reinforce the positive effects of treatment and minimize set-backs:
- physical activity (e.g. Can he start playing tennis again after this treatment?)
- self-care
- follow-up sessions with you
- follow-up sessions with primary care physicians.

Give the gift of awareness
- Follow client's process, how his/her function and symptoms improve over time.
- Advise that change and improvement does not always look like *the client expects*.
- Respond to the infamous phone call, "I'm not feeling any better."
- Help the client track and monitor his/her process and progress.
- Show him his progress when he is discouraged.
- Provide encouragement and reinforcement.

Validate changes (in relationships, work, health and other activities).
- Listen to changes in symptoms, which may mean progress and healing. State them as progress.

©1998 Ernesto J. Fernandez

Sample Client History Form

Date: _____ Name: _____

SS#: _____ Date of Birth: _____

Address: _____

City, State, Zip: _____

Home phone: _____ Work phone: _____

Marital Status (circle one): M S W D Sep.   # children _____

Employer: _____ Occupation: _____

Work Address: _____

City, State, Zip: _____

Name of Spouse: _____

Spouse's Employer: _____ Work phone: _____

Who referred you to this office? _____

Method of payment: Cash   Check

Who is responsible for payment (if not you)? _____

©1998 Ernesto J. Fernandez

Height _____ Weight _____ Age _____

Describe the health problems for which you came to see us.

_____

_____

How did this condition develop? When did it first start?

_____

_____

List diagnosis (if known) and treatment currently being used._____

_____

Describe the results from previous massage treatments for this condition. _____

Is there anything that makes your condition worse? _____

_____

_____

List all operations or illnesses. _____

_____

List all accidents, injuries or falls. _____

_____

If due to an auto accident, list date, and describe. _____

_____

Are you presently under a physician's care?   Y   N

If yes, please explain. _____

_____

What other healthcare practitioners have you seen for this condition? _____

_____

Please list present medications used and their purpose. ____

_____

Have you had surgery in past three years? Y   N

If yes, please explain. _____

Do you have any skin disorders or allergies? Y   N

If yes, please explain. _____

_____

Do you regularly drink caffeine beverages (coffee, tea, coke, etc)? Y N

Do you smoke? Y   N   If yes, how many packs a day? _____

Do you drink alcoholic beverages? Y   N   If yes, how much?

Are you pregnant? Y   N   If yes, what is the estimated due date? _____

Are you participating in a regular fitness program? Y   N

If yes, please describe. _____
_____

Do you have any other medical condition or physical
limitation that your therapist needs to be aware of before
you receive treatment? Y N

If yes, please explain: _____
_____

Circle all areas of pain.

	Head	
R. Shoulder	**Neck**	**L. Shoulder**
Arm	**Back**	**Arm**
Hand	**Chest**	**Hand**
	Abdomen	
Leg		**Leg**
Feet		**Feet**

Circle any of the following symptoms you experience.
Sometimes =S   Often = O   Past = P

Loose Stools/ Diarrhea	S O P	Cough	S O P
Flatulence	S O P	Shortness of breath	S O P
Vomiting	S O P	Decreased sense of smell	S O P
Belching/ Burping	S O P	Nasal problems	S O P
Heartburn	S O P	Skin problems	S O P
Feeling of distension	S O P	Bronchitis	S O P
after meals		Asthma	S O P
Tendency to be obsessive	S O P	Tendency to catch	S O P
in work, relationships		colds easily	
Fatigue	S O P	Intolerant to weather	S O P
Edema	S O P	changes	
Easily bruised	S O P	Allergies	S O P
Difficult to stop bleeding	S O P	Hay fever	S O P

©1998 Ernesto J. Fernandez

Irritable bowels	S	O	P
Constipation	S	O	P
Hemorrhoids	S	O	P
Blood in stools	S	O	P
Black stools	S	O	P

Low back pain			
Low back pain	S	O	P
Knee problems	S	O	P
Hearing impairment	S	O	P
Ringing in ears	S	O	P
Kidney stones	S	O	P
Decreased sex drive	S	O	P
Hair loss	S	O	P
Urinary problems	S	O	P

Eye problems			
Eye problems	S	O	P
Dizziness	S	O	P
Hepatitis	S	O	P
Difficulty digesting oily foods	S	O	P
Gall stones	S	O	P
Light colored stools	S	O	P
Soft or brittle nails	S	O	P
Easily angered or agitated	S	O	P

Insomnia, difficulty sleeping	S	O	P
Heart palpitations	S	O	P
Excessive dreaming			
Restless	S	O	P
Chest pains	S	O	P
Tendency to faint easily	S	O	P
High blood pressure	S	O	P

Difficulty making plans or decisions	S	O	P
Muscle spasm or twitching	S	O	P
Headaches	S	O	P
High cholesterol levels	S	O	P

Abdominal hernia	S	O	P
Arthritis	S	O	P
Sciatica	S	O	P
Bursitis	S	O	P
Blood clots	S	O	P
Broken bones	S	O	P
Hands/Feet - cold	S	O	P
Hand numbness	S	O	P
Cancer	S	O	P
Herniated Disk	S	O	P
Varicose veins	S	O	P
Loss of balance	S	O	P
Diabetes	S	O	P

Neck pain	S	O	P
P.M.S.	S	O	P
Severe menstrual pain	S	O	P
Severe irritability	S	O	P
Severe depression	S	O	P
Foot numbness	S	O	P
Carpal Tunnel Syndrome	S	O	P
TMJ (Temporal Mandibular Joint Disorders)	S	O	P

128

1. Because a massage therapist must be aware of any existing physical conditions that I have, I have listed all my known medical conditions and physical limitations and I will inform my massage therapist of any changes in my physical health.

2. I understand that:
a) the massage therapy that I am given is for the purpose of stress reduction, relief from muscular tension or spasm, and/or for improving circulation.

b) a massage therapist neither diagnoses illness, disease, or any other medical, physical or mental disorder; nor performs any spinal manipulations. I am responsible for consulting a qualified physician for any physical ailment I have.

3. I understand the information contained herein is privileged and confidential and at this time I authorize the release of any information pertaining to my health to my attorney, insurance company and/or physician(s)/therapist(s).

_____   _____

Signature   Date

Professional Associations

American Massage Therapy Association
820 Davis St., Ste. 100
Evanston, Illinois 60201-4444
(847) 864-0123

Associated Bodywork and Massage Professionals
P.O. Box 1869
Evergreen, CO 80439
(303) 674-8478

Florida State Massage Therapy Association
1089 W. Morse Blvd., Suite C
Winter Park, FL 32789
(407) 628-2772

National Certification Board for Therapeutic Massage
  and Bodywork
8201 Greensboro Dr., Ste. 300
McLean, VA 22102

International Association of Healthcare Practitioners
11211 Prosperity Farms Rd., Suite D325
Palm Beach Gardens, FL 33410-3487
(561) 622-4334

For a more comprehensive list of professional associations in the bodywork field refer to the Touch Training Directory, published by Associated Bodywork and Massage Professionals.

References and Suggested Reading

Supervision and Mentoring

Bernard, J. M. and Goodyear, R. K. (1992). Fundamentals of clinical supervision. Needham Heights, MA: Allyn and Bacon.

Drapela, V. J. (1983). The counselor as consultant and supervisor. Springfield: Charles C. Thomas.

Daloz, L. A. P. (1990). Mentorship. In: M. W. Galbraith (ed.), Adult learning methods: A guide to effective instruction (pp. 205-224). Malabar, FL: Krieger Publishing Company.

Hanks, K. (1991). Motivating People. Ontario: Crisp Publications.

Heider, J. (1985). The Tao of leadership: Leadership strategies for a new age. New York: Bantam.

Huang, C. A. and Lynch, J. (1995). Mentoring: the Tao of giving and receiving wisdom. San Francisco: Harper Collins.

Kauth, B. (1992). A circle of men: The original manual for men's support groups. New York: St. Martin's Press.

Loganbill, C., Hardy, E. & Delworth, U. (1982). Supervision: A conceptual model. The Counseling Psychologist, 10(1), 3-42.

Mezirow, J. et al. (1990). Fostering critical reflection in adulthood: A guide to transformative and emancipatory learning. San Francisco: Jossey-Bass.

Shea, G. F. (1992). Mentoring: A practical guide on how to develop successful mentoring behaviors. Menlo Park: Crisp Publications.

Sher, B. and Gottlieb, A. (1989). Teamworks! Building support groups that guarantee success. New York: Warner Press.

Florida Department of Business and Professional Regulation, Division of Professions: Board of Massage (October 1996) Laws and Rules Chapter 480, Florida Statues and Rule Chapter 61G11, Florida Administrative Code.

Post-Graduate Training

• *Theory*

Dychwald, K. (1977). BODYMIND. Los Angeles: Tarcher.

Painter, J. W. (1987). Deep bodywork and personal development: Harmonizing our bodies, emotions and thoughts. Mill Valley: Bodymind Books.

• *Evaluation and pathology*

Lowe, W. W. (1994). Functional assessment in massage therapy. Yachats: Pacific Orthopedic Massage.

Mercier, L. R. (1995). Practical orthopedics (4th ed.). St. Louis: Mosby.

Steinberg, G. G.; Akins, C. M.; & Baran, D. T. (ed.) (1992). Ramamurti's orthopaedics in primary care (2nd ed.). Baltimore: Williams and Wilkins.

Stolov, W. C. and Clowers, M. R. (ed.) (1981). Handbook of severe disability. Washington D.C.: Rehabilitation Services Administration.

Thompson, D. L. (1993). Hands heal: Documentation for massage therapy - A guide to SOAP charting. Seattle: Diana L. Thompson.

Vaughn, B. (1997). Functional assessment skills for massage therapists. Video.

• *Treatment*

Mattes, A. L. (1995). Active isolated stretching. Sarasota, FL: Aaron L. Mattes.

McCann, D. B. (1995). <u>A treatment manual of structural massage therapy</u>. Lutz, FL: Structural Energetic Therapy Institute.

Painter, J. W. (1987). <u>Technical manual of deep wholistic bodywork</u>. Mill Valley: Bodymind Books.

• *Anatomy and Physiology*

Juhan, D. (1987). <u>Job's body: A handbook for bodywork</u>. New York: Station Hill Press.

Sieg, K. W. and Adams, S. P. (1985). <u>Illustrated essentials of musculoskeletal anatomy</u> (2nd ed.). Gainesville: Megabooks.

Thibodeau, G. A. (1987). <u>Anatomy and physiology</u>. St. Louis: TimesMirror Mosby.

Therapeutic Relationships

• *Ethics*

Corey, G.; Corey, M. S. & Callanan, P. (1988). <u>Issues and ethics in the helping professions</u> (3rd ed.). Pacific Grove: Brooks/Cole.

Edge, R. S. and Groves, J. R. (1994). <u>The ethics of health care: A guide for clinical practice</u>. Albany: Delmar.

Leflet, D. H. (1995). <u>HEMME APPROACH to Ethics</u>. Bonifay: Hemme Approach Publications.

• *Consultation skills*

Aftel, M. and Lakoff, R.T. (1985). When Talk is Not Cheap. New York: Warner Books.

Balsam, R.M. (1984). Becoming a psychotherapist: A clinical primer. Chicago: University of Chicago Press.

Brammer, L.M.; Abrego, P.J.; Shostrom, E. L. (1993). Therapeutic Counseling and Psychotherapy (6th ed.). Englewood Cliffs: Prentice Hall.

Davies, C.M. (1989). Patient practitioner interaction: An experiential manual for developing the art of health care. Thorofare, NJ: SLACK.

Gladding, S.T. (1988). Counseling: A comprehensive profession. Columbus, OH: Merrill Publishing Co.

Gavin, J. and Gavin, N. (1995). Psychology for health fitness professionals. Champaign, IL: Human Kinetics.

Hepworth, D.H. and Larsen, J. (1986). Direct social work practice: Theory and skills. Chicago, IL: The Dorsey Press.

Johanson, G. and Kurtz, R. (1991). Grace unfolding: Psychotherapy in the spirit of the Tao-te ching. New York: Bell Tower.

Lukas, S. (1993). Where to start and what to ask: An assessment handbook. New York: W.W. Norton Press.

McNeely, D.A. (1987). Touching: Body-therapy and depth psychology. Toronto: Inner City Books.

Small, J. (1981). Becoming naturally therapeutic: A return to the true essence of helping. New York: Bantam.

Teyber, E. (1992). Interpersonal process in psychotherapy: A guide for clinical training (2nd ed.). Pacific Grove: Brooks/Cole.

Timms, R. and Connors, P. (1992). Embodying healing: Integrating bodywork and psychotherapy in recovery from childhood sexual abuse. Orwell, VT: Safer Society Press.

Whitfield, C.L. (1993). Boundaries and relationships: Knowing, protecting and enjoying the self. Deerfield Beach, FL: Health Communications, Inc.

Personal Empowerment

Berne, E. (1964). Games people play: The basic handbook of transactional analysis. New York: Ballantine.

Bly, R. (1988). A little book on the human shadow. San Francisco: Harper Collins.

Corey, G. (1986) I never knew I had a choice (3rd ed.). Monterey: Brooks/Cole.

Covey, S. R. (1989). The 7 habits of highly effective people: Powerful lessons in personal change. New York: Fireside.

Csikszentmihalyi, M. (1990). Flow: The psychology of optimal experience. New York: HarperPerrenial.

Danials, V. and Horowitz, L. J. (1976). Being and caring: A psychology for living (2nd ed.). Palo Alto, CA: Mayfield.

Evans, M. (1992) The ultimate hand book: Self-care for bodyworkers and massage therapists. San Francisco, CA: Laughing Duck Press.

James, M. and Jongeward, D. (1971). Born to win. New York: Signet.

Johnson, R. A. (1991). Owning your own shadow: Understanding the dark side of the psyche. San Francisco: Harper Collins.

Kepner, J. I. (1993). Body process: Working with the body in psychotherapy. San Francisco: Jossey-Bass.

Kottler, J.A. (1993). On being a therapist. San Francisco: Jossey-Bass.

Kurtz, R. and Prestera, H. (1984). The body reveals: What your body says about you. San Francisco: Harper and Row.

Lee, J. and Stott, B. (1993). Facing the fire: Experiencing and expressing anger appropriately. New York: Bantam.

Lowen, A. (1975). Bioenergetics: The revolutionary therapy that uses the language of the body to heal the problems of the mind. New York: Penguin Books.

Lowen, A. (1990). The spirituality of the body: Bio-energetics for grace and harmony. New York: Macmillan.

Moore, R. and Gillette, D. (1990). <u>King, warrior, magician, lover: Rediscovering the archetypes of the mature masculine</u>. San Francisco: Harper Collins.

Palmer, H. (1994). <u>Resurfacing: Techniques for exploring consciousness</u>. Altamonte Springs, FL: Star's Edge International.

Suggested Publications

Journal of Bodywork and Movement Therapies
1 (800) 553-5426

Massage Magazine
1 (800) 533-4263
1 (800) 872-1282